P9-DEL-963

~~Don't~~ Try This At Home!

Silly Circus Tricks

Nick Hunter

Raintree

Chicago, Illinois

© 2013 Raintree
an imprint of Capstone Global Library, LLC
Chicago, Illinois

To contact Capstone Global Library please phone 800-747-4992, or visit our website www.capstonepub.com

All rights reserved. No part of this publication may be reproduced or transmitted in any form or by any means, electronic or mechanical, including photocopying, recording, taping, or any information storage and retrieval system, without permission in writing from the publisher.

Edited by Rebecca Rissman, Daniel Nunn, and Adrian Vigliano
Designed by Cynthia Della-Rovere
Picture research by Elizabeth Alexander
Production by Alison Parsons
Originated by Capstone Global Library Ltd.
Printed and bound in China by China Translation and Printing Services Ltd.

16 15 14 13 12
10 9 8 7 6 5 4 3 2 1

Library of Congress Cataloging-in-Publication Data

Hunter, Nick.

 Silly circus tricks / Nick Hunter.

  p. cm.—(Try this at home!)

 Includes bibliographical references and index.

 ISBN 978-1-4109-5003-1 (hb)—ISBN 978-1-4109-5010-9 (pb) 1. Circus—Juvenile literature. 2. Tricks—Juvenile literature. I. Title.

 GV1817.H86 2013

 791.3—dc23   2012014405

Acknowledgments

The author and publisher are grateful to the following for permission to reproduce copyright material: Alamy p. 17 (© maxim.photoshelter.com); © Capstone Publishers pp. 7, 8, 9 t, 9 b, 10, 11, 12, 13 t, 13 b, 14, 15 t, 15 b, 16, 19 t, 19 b, 20 t, 21, 20 b, 22 t, 22 b, 23 t, 23 b, 26, 27 t, 27 b, 28, 29 (Karon Dubke); Getty Images pp. 5 (William West/AFP), 18 (Abdelhak Senna/AFP), 24 (Hannes Magerstaedt), 25 (Fotosearch); Shutterstock pp. 4 (© Hung Chung Chih), 6 (© michaeljung). Design features reproduced with the permission of Shutterstock (© Christophe Boisson), (© Merve Poray), (© Nicemonkey).

Cover photograph of a young woman juggling reproduced with permission of Corbis (© Ocean).

Every effort has been made to contact copyright holders of any material reproduced in this book. Any omissions will be rectified in subsequent printings if notice is given to the publisher.

All the Internet addresses (URLs) given in this book were valid at the time of going to press. However, due to the dynamic nature of the Internet, some addresses may have changed, or sites may have changed or ceased to exist since publication. While the author and publisher regret any inconvenience this may cause readers, no responsibility for any such changes can be accepted by either the author or the publisher.

Bloomington, Chicago, Mankato, Oxford

Contents

Some words are shown in bold, **like this**. You can find out what they mean by looking in the Glossary.

Roll Up! Roll Up!

Take a trip to the circus. You'll be amazed by the **acrobats** and **trapeze** artists flying high above your head. With a little bit of practice, you could amaze your friends with your own circus skills.

Big-top tip

Many circus tricks are highly dangerous and should only be performed by trained circus stars.

Amazing Acrobats

Acrobats make difficult and dangerous tricks look simple. If you want to be like them, it's important to stay safe when trying any new move. Check that you have something soft to land on.

A handstand is a great first move for a young acrobat.

Big-top tip

Make sure you **warm up** and stretch your **muscles** before trying any tricks. You don't want to pull a muscle when you're upside down.

The Handstand

Level of difficulty:
Easy

STEP 1

Start by kneeling at the wall. Put your hands flat on the floor about 12 inches (30 centimeters) from the wall.

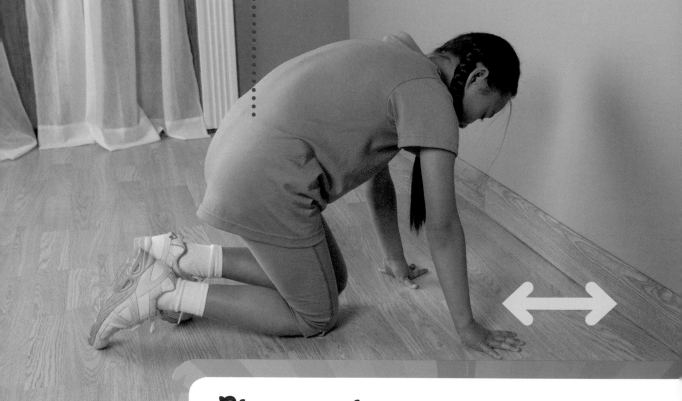

Big-top tip

Ask a friend to help you keep your legs straight and balance.

STEP 2

Straighten your legs to raise your hips into the air. Then kick one leg straight into the air until it's upright or resting on the wall.

STEP 3

Push your other leg into the air and point your toes. With practice, you'll be able to balance without the wall and even walk on your hands like a real circus **acrobat**.

Jazzy Juggling

Level of difficulty: Medium

Have you seen **jugglers** catching knives or even burning torches? Leave that to the experts. The best way to start is with just one ball.

Practice throwing the ball from one hand to the other. After a while, you should be able to catch it without even looking.

Big-top tip

Safety tips for first-time jugglers:

- Juggle with things that won't break (unlike this young juggler!).

- Clear some space so you don't knock things over.

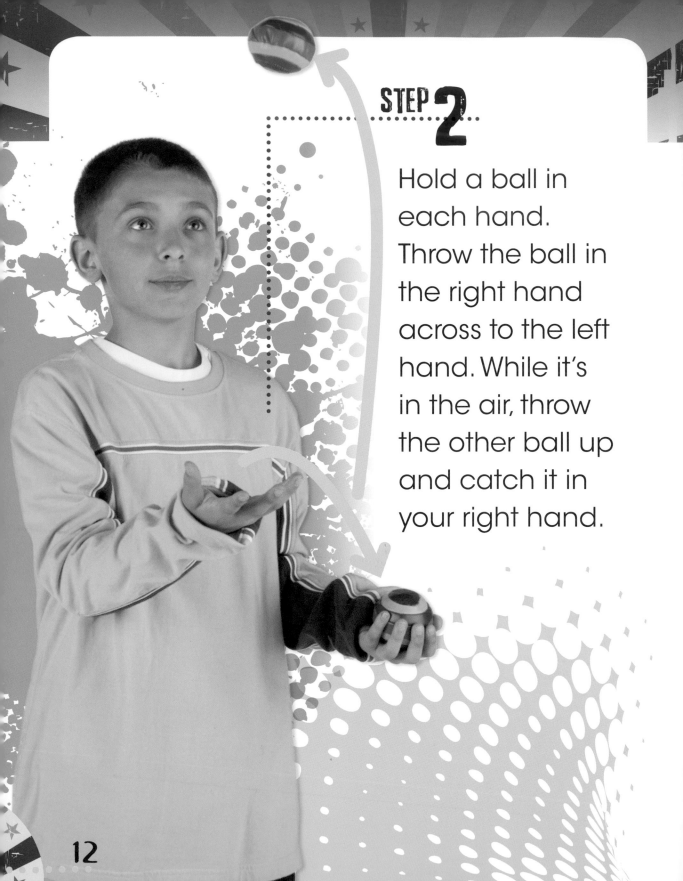

Hold a ball in each hand. Throw the ball in the right hand across to the left hand. While it's in the air, throw the other ball up and catch it in your right hand.

STEP 3

When you can juggle easily with two balls, add another one. Throw and catch them in order as before. You'll have to be quick, as one ball will always be in the air.

Big-top tip

Don't throw the balls too high. This will make it more difficult to catch them.

Stilt Crazy

Level of difficulty: Medium ⭐

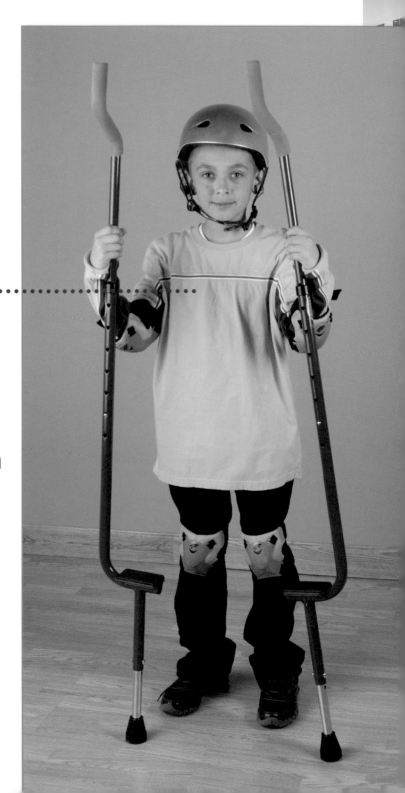

STEP **1** ············

How would you like to tower above your friends? You can start stilt walking with simple wooden **stilts**.

STEP 2

Your first challenge is standing up on stilts. It's easier to stand up if you start by sitting on a high seat, such as a stool or table.

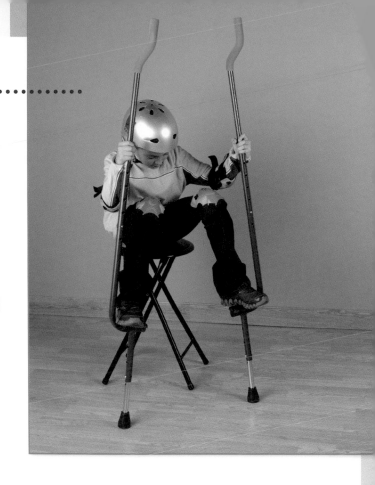

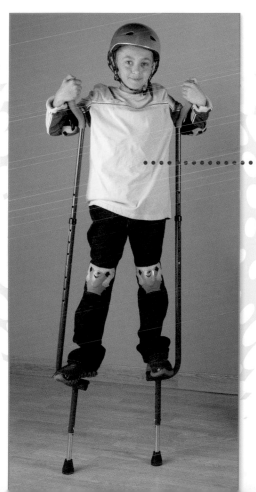

STEP 3

Once you're upright, stand as straight as you possibly can.

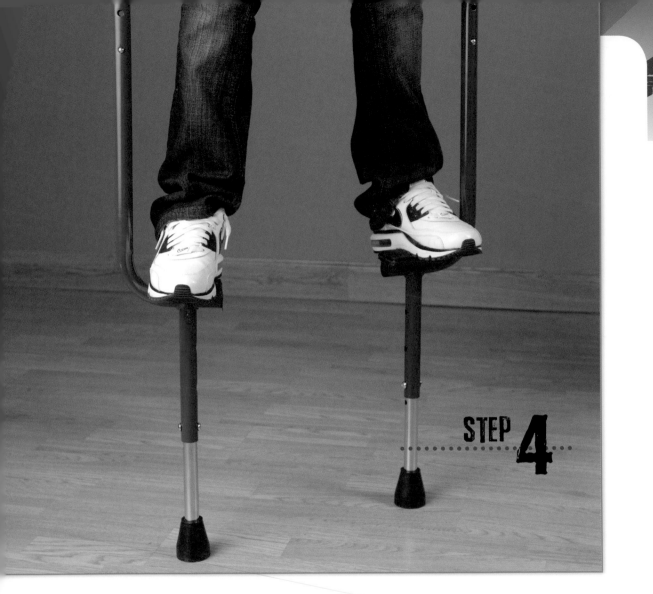

STEP 4

Practice marching in place with your stilts. Keep a wall or rope nearby to hold on to. Once you know you can keep your balance, try letting go. You can also upgrade to circus stilts that you strap onto your legs.

The circus is now just a few very big steps away.

Big-top tip

Make sure you wear equipment that will protect you if you fall over:

- bicycle helmet
- knee pads
- elbow pads or padded jacket

Walking a Tightrope

Level of difficulty:
Hard

Walking the high wire is one of the most amazing circus acts. It looks impossible. With a lot of hard work, you can do it.

Big-top tip

If you want to master this difficult trick, you'll have to put in hours of practice.

STEP 1

Tightrope walking is all about balance. Practice standing very straight on one leg. Then try doing it with your eyes closed.

STEP 2

Next, practice walking along a line on the ground. Try to keep your weight on the balls of your feet. Turn around without falling off the line.

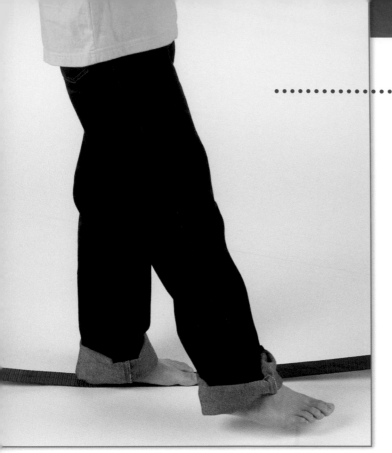

Now that you've got your balance, you can try standing on a slack rope. Bare feet will help you grip the rope.

STEP **4**

First, put one foot on the rope and try to stand for as long as possible. Start from the middle of the rope.

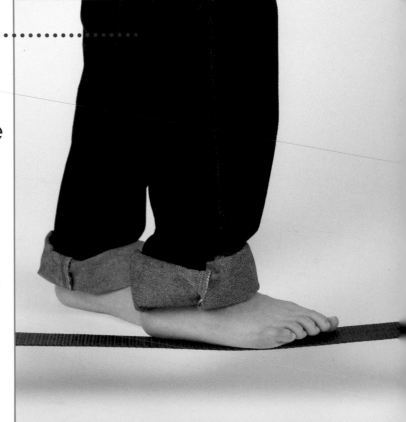

20

STEP 5

Keep your leg bent and point your foot along the rope. Using your other leg and spreading your arms will help you to balance.

Big-top tip

Start with a short rope close to the ground and a friend to help, so you won't end up with too many bruises.

STEP 6

If you can balance for several seconds, you're ready to try walking. Try placing your other foot on the wire in front of your standing foot.

STEP 7

Your weight usually goes onto your front foot. On a rope, keep your weight on the back foot as you put your front foot down.

22

STEP 8

When you get really good, you can turn around by placing your front foot across the rope. Twist around it so your back foot is facing the opposite way.

Big-top tip

If a friend sits on the rope, it will not move as much.

Clowning Around

It wouldn't be a circus without the clowns. It may look like they're just messing around, but clowns need skills to make people laugh and do clever tricks.

Crazy hair or a wacky wig

Painted face and a big red nose

The first thing you need is the right costume.

Brightly colored clothes that are far too big

Great big flappy shoes

Big-top tip
Don't forget funny **props**, like a plastic flower that squirts water.

Somersault

Level of difficulty:
Easy

Use the tricks you've already learned and add new ones. A simple **somersault** in a clown costume will have your audience laughing.

STEP **1**

Lean toward the ground. You could pretend you're tying your shoelace. Put your hands on the floor and curve your back.

Push with
your legs, so
that your weight
carries your legs
over your head.

STEP 3

Roll over, keeping
your back
curved, and
stand up again.

Showtime!

Now that you know the tricks, you can really put on a show. Give yourself a crazy name and find some great, sparkly clothes. Get your friends involved and pretend to be the **ringmaster**.

Big-top tip

Start your show with some easier tricks. You can build up to the most difficult and exciting acts, such as **tightrope** walking.

Glossary

acrobat someone who performs gymnastic tricks such as handstands and somersaults

juggler performer who can throw and catch several objects at once

muscle body part that makes your body move, such as by controlling your arms and legs

prop object used as part of a show or circus act

ringmaster person who introduces the acts at a circus and runs the show

somersault trick in which a person turns head over heels

stilts leg extensions made of wood or other material

tightrope rope or wire fixed between two points above the ground and pulled tight

trapeze narrow platform or swing high above the ground in a circus

warm up exercise to make sure your body is prepared for action and to prevent injuries

Find Out More

Books

Gifford, Clive and Chris Chaisty, *The Usborne Book of Juggling*, Usborne, 2009.

Meinking, Mary, *Who Walks the Tightrope? Working at a Circus* (*Wild Work* series), Raintree, 2010.

Nobleman, Marc Tyler, *Contortionists and Cannons: An Acrobatic Look at the Circus* (*Culture in Action* series), Raintree, 2010.

Internet Sites

Facthound offers a safe, fun way to find Internet sites related to this book. All of the sites on Facthound have been researched by our staff.

Here's all you do:

Visit www.facthound.com

Type in this code: 9781410950031

Index